SMART ~~DRUGS - THE~~ TRU NO

CW00867773

An Introductory Guide to Memory Enhancement, Cognitive Enhancement, and the Full Effects

Copyright 2015 by Colin Willis - All rights reserved.

This document is geared towards providing exact and reliable information in regards to the topic and issue covered. The publication is sold with the idea that the publisher is not required to render accounting, officially permitted, or otherwise, qualified services. If advice is necessary, legal or professional, a practiced individual in the profession should be ordered.

In no way is it legal to reproduce, duplicate, or transmit any part of this document in either electronic means or in printed format. Recording of this publication is strictly prohibited and any storage of this document is not allowed unless with written permission from the publisher. All rights reserved.

The information provided herein is stated to be truthful and consistent, in that any liability, in terms of inattention or otherwise, by any usage or abuse of any policies, processes, or directions contained within is the solitary and utter responsibility of the recipient reader. Under no circumstances will any legal responsibility or blame be held against the publisher for any reparation, damages, or monetary loss due to the information herein, either directly or indirectly.

The information herein is offered for informational purposes solely and is universal as so. The presentation of the information is without contract or any type of guarantee assurance.

The trademarks that are used are without any consent, and the publication of the trademark is without permission or backing by the trademark owner. All trademarks and brands within this book are for clarifying purposes only and are owned by the owners themselves, not affiliated with this document.

Table of Contents

Introduction

This book contains an overview of Nootropics, commonly referred to as smart drugs, as well as guiding information on cognitive and memory enhancement.

It is said that the human brain has almost limitless power in terms of cognition. Many past studies have revealed that, as human beings, we aren't truly using our brain's full potential. For many people, they fail to do this just because they aren't aware of how to unlock more of the brain's power. However, there are quite a few ways to do just that. Some choose to study up on the topic, while others get involved in mental training.

While such things can work to improve cognitive performance, these strategies require time, which many of us can't (or don't want to) really sacrifice. Luckily for us, the current availability of Nootropics helps to solve this dilemma. Yes, cognitive and memory enhancement through supplements is possible! It is currently the fastest way to enhance one's brainpower.

However, the kind of success that can be achieved through the use of smart drugs will depend upon correct and responsible use. There are right and wrong ways of cognitive enhancement through supplementation. Of course, you'd rather be on the right side of things for the sake of safety and maximum beneficial effects.

This is the primary reason why this book was put together. We hope to provide you sufficient knowledge regarding smart drugs, which will hopefully enable you to make wise decisions regarding its use. Information presented in each chapter has been kept simple yet concise so that you'll be on the path to successful cognitive enhancement as soon as possible.

We hope that you are able to learn a thing or two!

Chapter 1:

What Are Nootropics/Smart Drugs?

There is no doubt that brain power has always been something that people have been looking to improve - at least as soon as we could comprehend its limitless potential. This applies to people from all sorts of professions and walks of life. Brainpower determines how efficient and effective we can be in most aspects of our lives, and it is even being linked to the level of success that an individual can attain in his or her lifetime.

However, brainpower is not all about intelligence. It appears that the level of cognitive function is also a major measure of brainpower. Critical cognitive functions include memory, information processing, concentration, motivation, and many others.

With some conclusions being reached via research on the topics of brain plasticity and its chemical systems, a new area of interest has opened up. This new area of interest, even industry, is all about enhancing brain, or mental, power through a specific type of chemical. This is the study that is now being referred to as Nootropics by the mainstream. With the growing number of Nootropics being discovered these days, another name for this category of chemicals was born: "Smart Drugs."

People from different backgrounds have come up with their own names for Nootropics over the years. Some of the names that refer to it include memory enhancers, mental power boosters, neuro-enhancers, and brain pills. For technicality sake, Nootropics are chemicals that contain compounds that can boost cognitive functions. These substances are meant to have low toxicity levels, which are especially beneficial for long-term use.

The applications of Nootropics are not limited to the field of academics. These drugs are used openly in show, business, sports, medicine, military, and even in politics. Many new applications are being discovered these days. With the current literature and pioneering research projects being conducted about next-generation smart drugs, there is no doubt that more and more fields are going to benefit from it.

In general, Nootropics are organized into seven big categories. They are as follows:

Category A:

Natural/Herbal

These are chemical compounds that have been derived from plants. As long as the compound has properties that can improve mental or cognitive functions, it will be tagged as a Nootropic. One of the best herbal Nootropics out in the market today is Ginkgo Biloba. One thing to take note about Nootropics in this category is that the potency level is lower when compared to their synthetic counterparts.

Category B:

Racetams

Nootropics classified under this category all work with acetylcholine. This is a very important neural receptor that is linked to several cognitive functions such as recall, learning, and concentration. There are about 20 types of drugs under this category, but the most popular ones are Piracetam, Oxiracetam, and Aniracetam.

Category C:

Cholines

Cholines cannot work independently as Nootropics. Compounds under this category are "stacked" up, or combined, with those under the Racetams group. By doing this, enough acetylcholine can be produced by the brain cells for the best possible cognitive outputs. Centrophenoxine, Alpha GPC, Choline Bitartrate, and Citicholine are the most popular cholines on the market today.

Category D:

Peptides

Peptides are Nootropics that are noted for their high level of potency. Peptides are so potent that only small doses are recommended for users. As a best-case scenario, doses that are higher than what are prescribed to the use can produce uncomfortable side effects. In this worst-case scenario, large doses can become toxic.

Peptides are chemically similar to Racetams, which means that its capability to boost cognitive function is quite impressive. Noopept is the best example of a commercially available peptide that has been gaining acceptance from users all over the world today.

Category E:

Derivatives of Vitamin B

Nootropic products under this category work best against brain and body fatigue. There are only a few vitamin B (also referred to as b vitamin) derivatives out there, but it is relatively easy to find a product online and in pharmacies. Sulbutiamine is a name that most buyers will likely find in the market today.

Category F:

Ampakines

Ampakines are among the "next-generation" Nootropics. These are just recently developed and can boast impressive levels of strength as a neural function enhancer. There are glutamate receptors in the brain that are directly enhanced by Ampakines. It is to be noted that the glutamate receptor system plays a crucial role in the neuroplasticity property of the human brain - when this system receives a boost, the capacity for learning is increased.

Category G:

Smart Drugs

While Nootropics are also generally referred to as smart drugs by the mainstream, this category separates the two. Smart drugs are technically different because of the addition of stimulant properties. This means that problems that impair cognitive performance such as sleepiness, lack of "drive," and fatigue are solved initially.

When these problems are removed from the equation, cognitive enhancement can follow effectively and efficiently. Because of amphetamine derivation of newly developed and commercially available smart drugs, many types are heavily regulated. The best examples of these drugs are Modafinil and Adrafinil.

Chapter 2:

History of Nootropics

In a historical perspective, no one is really sure as to exactly when, where, and how people started using Nootropics. One thing is definite though: every culture and race had apparently found some use for substances derived from plants that could produce mind-altering effects.

Of course, our very distant ancestors didn't know that they were actually dealing with Nootropics. This term was coined a thousand years later, if we use the prehistoric periods as our point of reference.

So, what evidence have scientists used to determine the use of mind enhancing drugs during prehistoric times? Consider the following:

Caveman Drawings

Carbon dating reveals that there are cave drawings dating back to around 10,000 years ago. The figures on these drawings are similar to those seen by persons under the effect of psychoactive or mind-altering drugs. This likely indicates that these people tried to record what they saw under these altered states of consciousness.

South American Artifacts

There are bowls and tubes that have been unearthed that are alleged to have been used for preparing hallucinogens during rituals. These relics have been found in archeological sites near present-day Mexico. Carbon dating revealed that both the bowls and the tubes date back sometime between 100 and 400 BC!

There are other civilizations that have been recorded to be openly using plant-derived chemicals that can alter mood, motivation, and patterns of thinking. The Chinese, for example, have been known to use Ginkgo Biloba for many purposes, such as enhancement of concentration, memory improvement, boosting of physical strength, and others. This substance is now the basis of some modern products, which include memory pills, energy drinks, and even sex drive boosters.

The most notable and significant development in the history of mind enhancing substances just occurred recently. In the 1960's, a team of Belgian researchers, headed by Timothy Leary, conducted a study about psychedelic drugs. The aim of their research was to find a way through the blood-brain barrier so that the human consciousness could be expanded.

This meant synthesizing GABA (gamma-aminobutyric acid), which is a major neural inhibitor. The targeted product was a substance that could produce magnified GABA effects, such as stress reduction and relaxation. This was the time when the well-known Piracetam was discovered. Other research projects regarding the possible uses of Piracetam were launched during this time, though most ended in failure.

In the 1970's, the use of Piracetam for memory improvement was one of the most exciting highlights in recent medical history. It was during this period that the term "Nootropics" was coined. Dr. Corneliu Giurgea, a Romanian doctor, referred to Piracetam and other similar drugs as Nootropics, which meant "mind directing or mind bending" ("*nous*" and "*trepein*"). While Piracetam was discovered in the 1960's, it was in the 1970's that it was produced under the new category of Nootropics.

Dr. Giurgia came up with a set of guidelines as to what characteristics a drug or substance must have in order to be classified as a Nootropic. These included the following:

The substance must be able to stimulate memory and learning improvement.

The substance must produce memory and learning improvement that have better resistance to elements of disruption.

The substance must promote protection (physical and chemical) of the brain and its components.

The substance must support the improvement of control mechanisms of the brain (cortical and subcortical areas).

The substance must not have side effects that are produced by available psychotropic drugs.

The substance must have a toxicity level so low that it can be used safely over long periods of times (months or years).

Since the 1970's, more studies have been conducted to expand the horizons for Nootropic users and the medical community at large. One notable study sought to solve some of the symptoms of Alzheimer's disease through the use of Piracetam derivatives. More Nootropics were added to the Racetams category.

Some of the most well known are Aniracetam and Oxiracetam. There were also successful attempts to fuse choline with many of the already discovered Racetams.

As brain research yielded more information about the types of neurotransmitters, more Nootropics were developed. Modern-day Nootropics, or the rightful "Smart Drugs," are being combined with vitamin derivatives. The use of active and well-known stimulants, such as caffeine and nicotine, is prevalent in the same industry that develops and manufactures modern Nootropics.

While many of the modern Nootropics are readily available in pharmacies and nutritional supplement stores, a few types are tightly regulated. Examples of which include those that contain amphetamine derivatives as stacking components, but these are only available by prescription.

Even if this is the case, the acceptance for the use of smart drugs and Nootropics at large is increasing faster than anticipated. More and more breakthroughs on its forms and uses are being discovered.

Chapter 3:

The Science Behind Nootropics

With the definition of Nootropics being clearly specified in the previous chapters of this book, it is easy for one to think that they work in a simple manner. However, actually, the mechanism of Nootropics is a quite complicated one. For starters, the number of Nootropic drugs mentioned in Chapter 1 complicates the whole thing for an outsider looking in.

Each category and type of Nootropic works differently in terms of reaction with neural systems and the production of desired mental efficiency. Therefore, the basic question of *"How do Nootropics work?"* can have multiple answers. To better understand how they work, it is necessary for one to have a background, or a review, of how the human brain really functions.

Neurons (brain cells) make up the entire brain. Many vital cognitive functions, such as memory, thought organization, learning, and others, are dependent on the way that neurons communicate with each other. Communication is established mainly through an electro-chemical system, in which neurotransmitters are used. These are the chemicals that are released and received by the brain cells when communicating.

Additionally, there are many types of neurotransmitters. This already hints that each one of them has a specialized function(s). However, neurotransmitters can be categorized into two general groups based on their actions: excitatory and inhibitory neurotransmitters. The former boosts and encourages message transmission, while the latter slows down and prevents messages from being transmitted.

When a brain cell receives a message it releases a neurotransmitter. This binds with a specific receptor that is found on the other end of a synapse – the space between brain cells. The message is then conveyed to the next brain cell. This is the basic cycle of how the system works. It is to be noted that the neurotransmitter and the receptor to which it binds to are the primary components of this system. Essentially, Nootropics work by increasing the efficiency of this system.

Again, there are many such systems in the human brain. However, there are only four that are the most significant when it comes to cognitive functions: the dopaminic, serotonic, cholinergic, and glutamatergic systems. A brief discussion of each of these systems is provided below.

Dopaminic/Serotonic System

These two systems are commonly grouped as one because of the nature of the neurotransmitter components. Yes, dopamine and serotonin are the "feel-good hormones" that people commonly know about. These are important because of the feelings of pleasure and happiness that they can produce.

The dopaminic and serotonic systems make it possible for an individual to experience relaxation, upbeat moods, motivation, inspiration, rewards, and other similar feelings. It would be very clear that the effects of these systems are not directly related to cognitive functions.

However, research has proven that boosting the efficiency of these systems is needed to start and sustain significant developments in the cognitive performance of an individual. Those who are going to use dopamine-based supplements must take a word of caution seriously, as these could really become addictive and are not meant for daily use.

Cholinergic System

This system is based mainly on acetylcholine. Acetylcholine is a very powerful and essential neurotransmitter. It is needed for the health of the neurons' cell membranes. This neurotransmitter is the one that is needed primarily for important cognitive functions, such as learning, memory, sensory perception, and decision-making.

This system has nicotinic and muscarinic receptors. Nicotinic receptors react to the presence of the stimulant we all know about - nicotine. Muscarinic receptors have been named as such because of their reaction to the muscarine toxin from mushrooms, which can influence various changes in various physiological functions such as muscle contraction, heartbeat, breathing, and speed/quantity of release of other neurotransmitters.

Acetylcholine supplements are not enough to produce desired Nootropic effects. Racetams are often stacked up with cholines in order to achieve this. Generally, when this system is enhanced with Nootropics, it

speeds up the synaptic processes and increases the
amount of neurotransmitters released by each of the
brain's   systems.

Glutamatergic System

This system is based mainly on the neurotransmitter called glutamate. This happens to be the most abundant neurotransmitter and can be converted into another substance called GABA. The glutamatergic system is responsible for the correct and efficient functioning of the brain, brain cell health, and the promotion of major cognitive faculties, such as learning and memory (both short and long-term).

Normal glutamate levels in the system and in the brain should be maintained. The sensitivity of the brain to these levels is so great that it wouldn't work efficiently if there were excess or deficient amounts of glutamate. The neurotransmitter easily becomes toxic as well.

In terms of available receptors that can complete the system, there are plenty to find. However, only two have been identified when it comes to the purpose of boosting up the cognitive functions of an individual: the NMDA and AMPA receptors. The majority of the Nootropic products available in the market today target these specific receptors. Those who want to boost up their cognitive functions often pick Ampakines and/or Racetams.

As mentioned above, Nootropics have varied effects on the brain. The mechanism of action can be different with each type of smart drug. However, there is usually only one result that people are after: a heightened level of cognitive performance that doesn't come with side effects.

The effects of Nootropics are scientifically validated and backed up with years of research. While there are still ongoing research projects regarding the details of its "negligible" side effects, the future of Nootropics is undoubtedly bright.

Chapter 4:

The Effects of Nootropics

Yes, Nootropics can undoubtedly make a person smarter, happier, and more efficient. However, those who are wise enough to know the price of artificial enhancement will demand more details. Ever since the first Nootropics were discovered, society has been interested in knowing its short and long-term effects.

Unfortunately, the field of Nootropics research is not yet that expansive. While classic Nootropics, most specifically Piracetam, have been researched well, the same cannot be said for those that belong to other categories. Current research is either aimed at developing new types of smart drugs or designing stacking combinations that suit specific purposes.

The good news is that if some of those Nootropics that were discovered a few years ago are used as a point of reference, some generalizations about their effects will be clear. By combining information from notes of researchers and the reviews of Nootropic users, the following can safely be derived:

Short-Term Effects

The effects of Nootropic pills will vary from one person to another. This is in terms of the speed and intensity of effects. This is understandable if individual physiological factors are taken into consideration. Age, sensitivity to medications, level of mental and physical activity, and even a person's health status are all examples of these factors.

For many people, effects can be felt within an hour or two after ingesting the pills. For some, observable effects can be felt after a couple of days from the intake of Nootropics. There are many descriptions as to how short-term Nootropic effects are manifested. However, one of the most observable effects, as narrated by users, is improvement in sensory perception. Many users of Piracetam, in reviews, have reported the following improvements in their level of sensory perception:

Sounds can become more distinct. There is an ability to notice even small changes in the sounds that one has become accustomed to hearing. Listening to music and the sounds of nature can become more enjoyable.

The identification of specific smells is easier. This gives way to better appreciation of the world through the different aromas that are present.

Quality of sight can improve significantly. Colors can be more vibrant and distinct, and images are often perceived to be brighter than usual.

Another very observable effect of Nootropic intake is the heightened level of eye and body coordination. There are people who report that they find it easier to use computer keyboards, ride bikes, and other similar activities that require a bit of dexterity.

Speech can also improve. There are those who have noted a marked improvement in their impromptu speaking abilities.

In general, all types of Nootropics can boost up the mental performance of an individual. This covers the ability to concentrate on mental tasks, perform tasks for longer periods of time, and maintain mental clarity in spite of physical and mental distractions. These abilities, when combined, give a person great power to outperform others in many types of activities, academic or non-academic.

It is also necessary to include memory enhancement as one of the best short-term effects of Nootropics. Of course, this only pertains to short-term memory. Users often report that it is easier for them to remember and retain information. Reasoning skills come with the power to remember things. These are of course very useful for those who are in the field of academics or are students.

As a plus factor for the short-term effects of Nootropics, users can have their stress levels lowered. Stress has long been identified as one of the biggest inhibitors of good cognitive performance. Nootropics make use of "feel good hormones" as an important component. This is especially true of the most recently developed Nootropics today. This is what makes these pills an "all in one" solution for the needs of many users.

Long-Term Effects

Long-term effects can be felt when one uses Nootropic medications that are designed for continuous consumption. The long-term effects are a result of the stacking up of short-term benefits and changes in the actual neural system. There is a definite list of long-term effects that could be enjoyed by those who use Nootropics over a prolonged period of time. They include the following:

Capability to support fast and robust brain cell growth. This also means the prevention of brain aging. The aging process comes with symptoms such as forgetfulness, slowness of processing power, and a decline in the power of eye and body coordination.

Increased level of brain health. Neurotransmitters that are produced through supplementation could back up the health of neural cell membranes. This means longer lives for the brain cells. The process of neuroplasticity is also supported when the brain is at its peak level of health. More connections between brain cells as a result of supplementation give additional learning power. Long-term memory is also boosted.

Better capability for healing when the brain is physically or chemically injured. Many research results show the effectiveness of Nootropics in treating both early and late symptoms of Alzheimer's. This could also be attributed to the power of Nootropics to enhance the growth factor of brain cells, as mentioned above.

Side Effects

Just like the many medications that are in use today, Nootropics are generally safe, but this doesn't mean they are free of side effects. Current research has shown that the use of Nootropics can cause certain side effects. The possible side effects include the following:

Gastrointestinal Troubles

These include diarrhea, stomach pain, and other similar symptoms. Of course, these symptoms rarely occur. Such troubles often arise when there are excessive amounts of Nootropics ingested. This typically happens when normal doses are exceeded, or when an individual is experimenting with stacking up different types of Nootropics.

Headaches

The majority of those who have participated in surveys and testimonial drives have reported headaches as a common side effect. This is easy to explain. Headaches arise when the brain's supply of neurotransmitters get depleted. It is to be noted that one of the actions of Nootropics is to stimulate the brain to produce and release more neurotransmitters, like acetylcholine, than it normally does.

Supplementing the neurotransmitter supply is usually the easiest solution here. Cholines that are stacked up with other Nootropics can solve the problem.

Unusual tiredness, insomnia, and irregular heartbeat

It is to be noted that Nootropics put the brain in a "hyper" mode. The heightened activity levels require a lot of energy that can drain up the normal supplies of the body. When the effect of the pill fades away, it is common for the entire human body to have no more extra energy or neurotransmitters to sustain the "high."

This often results in feelings of extreme fatigue, the inability to sleep, and irregularity of heartbeat. The easiest solution here is for an individual to take dopamine supplements or other types of pills that have those "feel good hormones" as an ingredient.

To summarize it all, Nootropics have short and long-term effects that users can enjoy. With these benefits also come some side effects that early literature about Nootropics failed to mention. Fortunately, these side effects are not as serious as what some people might fear. Additionally, a lot of effective solutions have been found to cope with these side effects. Knowing the benefits and side effects can help people decide whether or not to use Nootropics.

Chapter 5:

Pros and Cons of Smart Drugs

Are Nootropics right for me? This is a common question that many people will have on their minds if they have gotten to this chapter. While the nature, benefits, and effects of Nootropics have been clearly described already, many can't seem to make up their minds unless they really weigh the pros and cons. Because the mode of action of Nootropics can vary, coming up with a comprehensive list can be tricky.

For beginners, it is best to look at the most obvious pros and cons that many online reviews and research has provided.

Pros

Enhanced productivity levels

Nootropics improve mental focus, provide more energy, and can increase motivation. Overall, they increases productivity.

Ease of access to products

Nootropic products, except those that contain amphetamine derivatives, can be easy to find. There are many licensed online shops and brick and mortar stores that sell smart drugs without any special requirements or prescriptions.

Minimal side effects

When consumed properly and in the correct dosage, Nootropics can be considered fairly safe. Side effects tend to appear only if users deviate from the prescribed intake and stacking (blending).

Cons

Quality of effects may vary from person to person

Some people may experience immediate effects after intake. However, there are some who have to wait a few days before noticing any observable effects. In some instances, dosage adjustments need to be made in order to bring about beneficial effects.

Failure in drug tests

This is most true for those who are taking Adderall and/or Ritalin, as these contain amphetamine derivatives. Those who are consuming them could fail specific drug tests. It should also be noted that these types of Nootropics could be addictive, which is why they are designed for short-term use only.

Bitter taste

The majority of all the Nootropics found in the market today have an outright bitter taste. As an example, Piracetam tastes very unpleasant even in its pill form. The most common solution here is to mask the taste with a sweetened juice or other type of beverage.

Some are hard to find

There are types of smart drugs that are just too difficult to find in local pharmacies and supplement stores. One of the best examples is Modafinil. The rare types of Nootropics are usually those that are marked as "special blends" and are sold exclusively by online retailers.

Cost

When it comes to Nootropics, people can go cheap or pay the extra cost to get the more expensive brands. Classic Nootropics, like Racetams, are often the most inexpensive because of availability. Designer brands and special blends are usually the priciest. Of course, based on the experiences of many users, Nootropics for short-term use are usually fairly inexpensive. Computing the price of Nootropics on a "per serving" basis gives a more accurate view as to whether a specific type is cheap or pricey.

As Racetams are known to be inexpensive, a price ranking has been prepared below to serve as an example. Take note that the figures presented are the cheapest ones seen online. The actual price could vary depending on manufacturer, seller, point of sale, and other factors.

Rank 1: Piracetam - $39.99 per 500g package or $0.31 per serving (4 grams)

Rank 2: Noopept - $39.99 per 10g package or $0.16 per serving (40 milligrams)

Rank 3: Pramiracetam - $59.99 per 50g package or $0.48 per serving (400 milligrams)

Rank 4: Aniracetam - $17.99 per 50g package or $0.72 per serving (2 grams)

Rank 5: Oxiracetam - $29.99 per 50g package or $0.96 per serving (1.6 grams).

Smart pills, or those that specifically belong in the "Smart Drugs" category, as described in Chapter 1, are more expensive. Three examples have been provided below:

Addie Up: $59.99/bottle or $1.99 per serving (1 pill) – A stimulant mix, and not a true Nootropic.

Excelerol: $99.00/bottle or $3.33 per serving (1 pill) – An ingredient-packed supplement that boasts of Nootropic/Stimulant effects.

TruBrain: $125.00/bottle or $4.16 per serving (1 pill) – A mix of Piracetam, DHA, CDP Choline, ALCAR, theanine, and other cognitive performance boosters.

With the pros, cons, and costs of Nootropics presented clearly in this chapter, anyone can now make an informed decision as to whether or not they would like to consume them.

Chapter 6:

Classic Nootropics Compared to Recently Developed Smart Drugs

Let's compare the "classics" with some of the most recently developed Nootropics. By classics, experts are referring to the first Nootropics discovered. The information available on these drugs is a good reference point when making comparisons.

For this matter, one could compare members of Racetams (Category B) and Smart Drugs (Category G). Piracetam is the perfect sample for Category B because it was the first Nootropic to be discovered. Modafinil fits perfectly as the comparison partner of Piracetam. Basically, these are the most common options for anyone using brain enhancers for the first time. The following points of comparison should shed light on the similarities and differences between these two cognitive performance enhancers:

Mode of Action:

Piracetam utilizes glucose metabolism and improves blood and oxygen supply to brain cells. Cognitive function is supported through the enhancement of muscarinic cholinergic, AMPA, and NMDA receptors. Benefits are labeled as weak to moderate. It does not support any particular cognitive function, only general functions.

Modafinil utilizes its power to amplify histamine levels in the brain. With this type of change, mental energy, wakefulness, and motivation to perform in cognitive tasks are noticeably boosted. These are elements that give this drug very powerful Nootropic effects.

This drug is often prescribed as a narcoleptic agent. It enables an individual to be productive by getting rid of the effects of lack of sleep and fatigue. Benefits of Modafinil are marked highly when compared to those of early Racetams.

Potency:

Piracetam is quite potent when the recommended dosages are followed. The dosage range is from 1,000 to 6,000 milligrams. Users report observable effects being felt within a couple of hours from intake, but it may vary according to individual sensitivities.

Comparably, Modafinil, and all other members of Category G, are highly potent. Maximum desirable effects are felt even when using lower dosages. The recommended dosage range is from 100 to 400 milligrams only.

Duration of Effect:

The best approach when comparing the duration of effects of Nootropic drugs is to look at the value of individual half-lives. The figure states how long the active substances stay in the body and provide the desired effects. Classic Racetams usually have relatively short half-lives.

Piracetam can stay in the system and have its effects last for 4-5 hours. For many modern Category G drugs, half-lives are considerably longer. Modafinil can stay active within the body for 12 to 15 hours.

Risks and Side Effects:

Classic Racetams are known to have very minimal or no side effects at all. The appearance of side effects may depend upon dosage and sensitivity to the active components of the drug. Reported rare side effects from use of Piracetam include headache, weakness, insomnia, gastrointestinal tract irritation, and increased sexual appetite (libido).

Category G drugs are known to have more pronounced side effects. Side effects that are more likely to be experienced by all users include headache, nausea, anxiety, and hand tremors. Also, overdosing is a great risk for users. A Modafinil overdose is characterized by an extremely fast heartbeat, inability to sleep, panic attacks, and elevated blood pressure. There is also a greater risk of addiction for users. This is the reason why most Category G Nootropics are tightly regulated. Modafinil, Adderall, Adrafinil, and others are available only by prescription.

Cost:

Piracetam is quite cheap. However, there are even Racetams that can be on the expensive side. Based on the data presented in the previous chapter, people only need to spend $0.31 per dose ($39.99/bottle) on Piracetam powder. Phenylpiracetam is available on a price range of $18.99 to $238.99 per bottle.

Because Category G drugs are regulated and more potent, they are on the more expensive side. Modafinil can be purchased at $2.00 per pill outside United States territories, but there are verified reports that some Modafinil variations have reached the $50.00/pill price mark. Generic variations are in the price range of $543.00 to $560.00 per 100 mg pack. Branded variations, like Provigil, are available at $800.00 to $990.00 per 100 mg pack.

It is easy to see the wide differences between classic Nootropics and modern smart drugs. While there are exciting benefits that each option can offer, there are also risks that need to be considered and carefully weighed. The availability of many options when it comes to Nootropics is a privilege that everyone must use   responsibly.

Chapter 7:

The Future of Smart Drugs

Even though man's quest for brain or memory enhancing compounds has already produced many successes, things haven't stopped yet. There are studies and experiments being conducted that may shape the future and further use of smart drugs. This mainly because this is a class of Nootropics that is more potent, less risky, and can produce long-term health benefits. Currently, Ampakines are being referred to as the future of smart drugs. Also, there is the promise that this Nootropic class can achieve what some of earlier smart drugs failed to do.

On a more technical side, Ampakines work on the AMPA (α-Amino-3-hydroxy-5-methyl-4-

isoxazolepropionic acid) and NMDA (N-Methyl-D-aspartic acid) receptors through the stimulation of glutamate. It should be noted that glutamate is a vital neurotransmitter that can affect synaptic transmission speed and quality.

An interesting thing about these receptors is that newly developed Ampakines could get them intensely modulated. To take things up another notch, some of today's researchers have found an "intelligent modulation mechanism" in the brain that can be developed through short-term exposure to Ampakines. This means that the receptors would adjust its heightened level of function only when a certain need arises.

The medical field is also interested on the possible benefits of new Ampakines for individuals who are suffering from ADHD, Alzheimer's, and dementia. Another advantage of Ampakines is that the side effects that commonly come with use of other Nootropics and stimulants are totally eliminated. Earlier claims that Ampakines (like Sunifiram) are up to 1,000 times more potent are true, which indicates the need for lower dosages and of a reduced risk of toxicity.

Ampakines currently available on the market include the following:

Sunifiram

Very effective in stimulating glutamate levels in the brain. It can boost the memory and information processing speed of the brain. Effects of Phenylpiracetam are mirrored effectively.

Colouracetam

A hybrid racetam that is also categorized as an Ampakine. This drug improves both the brain and body for optimal cognitive performance. It produces the same effects that Phenylpiracetam and Modafinil can produce.

Unifiram

The chemical composition and effects of this drug is identical to that of Sunifiram. However, it is pricey because of its availability is limited on the market.

There are also Ampakines that are still under research and development. Those that are worthy of being mentioned include the following:

CX-516

This has already been given the name *Ampalex*. It is designed to be a drug that can put one's memory, learning, and focus in hyper mode. Other applications being explored include the treatment of Alzheimer's and ADHD (children and adults).

LY-404187

This drug is designed mainly to act on AMPA receptors. It gives an individual an increased capability to encode and recall memories. The capability of it to help individuals with schizophrenia, Parkinson's, chronic depression, and ADHD is still being researched.

CX-717

Developers of this drug have focused on its ability to boost cognitive performance and memory much faster than other Ampakines available on the market. It is also being developed as a long-term solution for ADHD and Alzheimer's. Trial runs have revealed CX-717 to be very effective in countering the effects of lack of sleep. This makes it a promising type of Ampakine for those who need top cognitive and physical performance during night shifts at work.

With the types of benefits that could be enjoyed by users, there is no doubt that the popularity of Ampakines will continue to rise. Research on new types of Ampakines also brings people closer to understanding the detailed "blueprint" of the human brain. While so much of the human brain is still mysterious, this will help us to harness the brain's power to higher levels. However, of course, this comes with the assurance that there will be minimal or no risk at all to the health of an individual.

Conclusion

Thank you for reading this! We hope this short, concise book was able to teach you a thing or two about Nootropics.

Now that you understand the important factors regarding Nootropics, you can decide if you want to try it, or if you can inform your friends who ask you about it. Plus, a little addition to your knowledge doesn't hurt, right? Our world is becoming increasingly interested in the use of Nootropics, in hopes to enhance the human experience on Earth.

If you've learned anything from this book, please take the time to share your thoughts by sending me a personal message, or even posting a review on Amazon. It would be greatly appreciated and I try my best to get back to every message!

Thank you and good luck in your journey!

27279180R00046

Printed in Great Britain
by Amazon